Railway of Rice

Railway of Rice

William Shoobridge

The Pentland Press Limited
Edinburgh • Cambridge • Durham • USA

First published in 1995 by
The Pentland Press Ltd.
1 Hutton Close
South Church
Bishop Auckland
Durham

British Library Cataloguing in Publication Data.
A catalogue record for this book is available
from the British Library.

ISBN 1 85821 308 8

All photographs reproduced by
the kind permission of the
Imperial War Museum

Typeset by CBS, Felixstowe, Suffolk
Printed and bound by Antony Rowe Ltd., Chippenham

PREFACE

As I reflect on my experience as a Far East P.O.W. and the possible repercussions that could have ensued, my views fifty years later, are completely different from those I held during my captivity. My reasons for this are simple: naturally, at the time things were pretty grim, but that period of nearly four years has been completely overwhelmed by fifty years of contentment and happiness. There are many people who tend these days to be discontented, and are often prepared to run our country down, they cannot seem to face up to a mild crisis without some sort of drug. I am fortunate, for I see life in a completely different perspective. The sad thing I often reflect upon, is the number of really decent friends I saw waste away, whom I had to bury or burn, chaps who wouldn't do anyone a bad turn; nowadays there are young muggers around who attack defenceless old folk, and are usually let off with a light sentence. The old saying, 'You find out the hard way' is mostly true, and there is only one person who can make you happy and contented during your life and that is yourself, for if you want to take the view you've got plenty of troubles, then bet your life you always will have plenty. I also believe that many people today think wealth and prosperity are the priorities of life, but alas, there are few who will be satisfied and content. Many times on the railway I dreamt I was home, to be awakened by the stench of bugs, lice, and fellow prisoners you couldn't help in any way, to struggle across in the dawn light to get your pint of sloppy rice for breakfast, one 'Jimmy Riddle and it had gone'. Disappointing, especially if you were sitting down having a tasty meal in your dream.

Whereas now, on occasions I still dream I'm back on the railway, but what a lovely feeling to wake up and realise you're in clean sheets and a soft bed, with your wife and in a free country, although many would not agree with this. But for the rest of my life these and many other little things, to me will be priceless.

Comradeship I suppose, was at its greatest; considering the conditions and stresses, I do not believe it would be possible, for a community of men to live in better harmony than we did. Looking back I think the main reason for this was due to the fact that we were all in it together, and we all had nothing. I don't believe you could get the same harmony and friendship in civilian life even if you all had the same amount of wealth and belongings. Once there is something around the old trouble of greed creeps in, and a few get dissatisfied.

Weighing up the experience I must say that now I'm positive that it was a valuable help to me, and the bond and friendship amongst all survivors is as great as ever. The Japanese tried all they could to humiliate and degrade the white P.O.W. from the so-called capitalist west. I detected an envious view towards us.

Since being financed by the Americans after the war, they couldn't get into the Westerly trend quickly enough in dress, way of life and capitalism, even spending millions on trying to buy the best bloodstock in Europe.

People who have visited Japan since the war have said what great hospitality and politeness they have shown. They have been professionals at that for centuries, they can bow and raise their hats for ever, I'm afraid it will not change my views of them. There are too many people in this world who take the view that if they say sorry, after bashing your brains out, that makes it all right.

Of course there must have been some good, there must be in all races. But if the good have allowed the wicked to take them over, and lead them into savage and inhumane treatment of other humans for their ultimate gain, then they also are as bad. One thing often struck me as strange, to see many senior Japanese officers ordering brutal treatment to British P.O.W. and yet still proudly wearing their British medal ribbons they were awarded as our allies in the Great War.

The old saying, 'forgive and forget' sounds good in theory, but I don't know what age you have to live to for this to take place. If we were threatened again as in 1939, I would still be prepared to join up. We have our faults, but there is no other country in the world to compare with this when you weigh up the basic facts.

FOREWORD
by
Group Captain Harold W. Whittingham, M.A., M.B., BCh., M.R.C.S., L.R.C.A., D.T.M. & H., R.A.F. Retd.

Little did I think that in a pretty brick cottage up a narrow lane in this small Herefordshire village lived a man with such a tale.

In six years I have got to know Bill Shoobridge, to admire his Cockney character, humour and philosophy of life. Bill was born in Tottenham on 3rd March, 1922, into a working-class family. As a schoolboy he worked on market stalls and in Covent Garden. He even learnt to resole his boots! His sports included football, boxing and cross-country running, which he shared with his father.

When war threatened he joined the Royal Artillery on his 17th birthday as a Gun Artificer. He serviced heavy anti-aircraft guns over an area north of the Thames from the Isle of Dogs to Hertfordshire. As only a private, his skill put him in charge of a gun-repairing team. During the blitz his transport was a Carter Paterson van!

In November 1941 the best men in his trade were required for service in the East, and a 10-weeks' troopship voyage took him to Singapore as a young Sergeant, where his story begins.

His arrival coincided with the fall of Singapore on 15th

February, 1942, and ends with his release from P.O.W. captivity in August, 1945.

His story, told in Cockney style with Cockney humour, speaks for the man. It is a lesson in survival under atrocious tropical conditions and brutal captors. It is yet another tale of man's inhumanity to man.

From his capture, Bill was determined to survive. To do this he had to forget home and family and concentrate solely on surviving from day to day. There was to be no self-pity, but plenty of very hard work to occupy his mind. He helped his comrades when he could and spread his philosophy of survival.

Bill passed an ultimate test of a man's calibre, 'guts', self-sufficiency and will-power.

This is a tribute to a great Cockney.

Harold Witherington

Railway of Rice

Silence fell upon the battered island of Singapore. The red sky of burning fuel dumps and vehicles still glowed, with huge explosions rocking the earth as great containers reached their ultimate heat. 8.30 pm the time, 15th February 1942, not one of the most prominent dates in history, but to me a date to be remembered for life.

Men gathered in groups, some tearful, many bewildered by what the future held in store for them. Myself, a nineteen year old Sergeant, thought little about the future at that time, but I must admit I was looking forward to a night's sleep as during the past few weeks this had become a rarity. All arms had to be discarded and piled in heaps, and most chaps were content to doze where they were.

The morning arrived with utter confusion. Japanese soldiers were buzzing around like blue arsed flies and putting signs on certain buildings and warehouses, mounting guards at strategic points. During this time we removed the breeches of four, 3.7 AA guns, making them useless, and loaded them into a truck which we drove with caution to a bridge patrolled by Japanese sentries. Waiting until they were in a blind position, we quickly struggled to slide them into the thick muddy bank of the river, we knew what to expect if we had been spotted.

We returned to our unit feeling quite pleased with our first day in captivity. By mid morning my O.C. informed me that the Japanese had ordered all P.O.W.s to rendezvous at Changi. The latter part of the campaign had been chaotic as far as rations were concerned, and as I had previously found a cold storage depot full of a good selection of food, I suggested that we loaded a couple of wagons to take with us to Changi. He proposed that his second in command should come with me and see the food. On arriving at the depot I opened several storage doors to show him. He didn't agree with me at first that it was right to take it, but after a little persuasion he saw my point. I quickly got the lads out to load up. I forgot to mention the Japanese had put their sign on this building and patrols were guarding the perimeter. But still we managed to load up and were out like a dose of salts. We had already had a few weeks' practice at loading up rations pronto.

Since the naval base had been evacuated a few weeks before, we had gone daily to replenish our food stocks there. At that time the Japanese were still on the mainland, and they could see us visiting. In spite of an unwelcome barrage of fire, we managed to slip away unscarred on each occasion. Later that afternoon we arrived at Changi village after a four hour march, the main bulk of the troops were to be housed in the barrack blocks, but Argylls and us were to stay in Changi village and live in the old Chinese wooden shanty type shops. Life continued here for a couple of months, more or less under our own administration, and apart from a barbed perimeter fence which circled the whole of Changi and the sight of an occasional Japanese truck passing through, or taking out working parties of P.O.W. to work in Singapore docks or the building of a shrine, we were left alone, totally unaware of their future plans to build a supply railway through to Burma for their troops. This had, apparently, been dismissed by the British and Americans before the war as being an impossibility even with the use of modern equipment. They reckoned it would be at much too great a cost of life.

We used to arrange a weekly concert in an old open air cinema. I usually participated with a rendering of Harry Champion. The rations of tinned food quickly began to dwindle, and more and more we survived on a diet of rice. All this time most of us seemed to suffer from acute constipation. I remember each day came and passed; finally after twenty-eight days I went on sick parade, and the doctor said if I did not go within a fortnight he'd give me half a number 9. Within that fortnight we couldn't dig bore holes quickly enough as everybody switched to dysentery. Most of us still had cash as we had received wages up until hostilities ceased, and we had had no chance of spending it. Little parties of smugglers sprang up. We would get out of the camp and rendezvous with natives, mostly at night; they would steal food from the warehouses in Singapore and fetch it up to their jungle huts, where we would barter with them. On occasions they would do us over, steal our cash, then we would catch them coming Indian file through the tracks and relieve them of their goods. Several times we had personnel killed by Sikh guards who had been fighting with us, but had gone over to the Japanese and were the perimeter guards.

By this time, we had learnt many ways to cook rice including grinding it down to make flour, making rissoles and frying in Vaseline of which I had acquired a large tin. Suddenly we were informed that a party of 600 were required in Siam as a working force and I was included. We were transported to Singapore station with our few belongings which by this time didn't amount to much. We were herded into enclosed steel trucks with just enough room to stand, and we began to roll. The local Malaysians, being quite friendly, began lobbing coconuts, bananas and pineapples through half a door that was left open for air. Before many miles at a speed of around 10 to 15 miles an hour, we began to have more pineapples than men; as we were pretty hungry we ate rather more than was good for us, and we were soon taking turns to hang our backsides out the door; our lips were raw with the acid. Numerous stops occurred for wood and water. Each time there would be a trail of chaps crouched on the line, then there was a frantic scramble to catch up the train when it continued its journey. After four days of stopping and starting we arrived at the small Thai village called Bang Pong which is just over the Malayan border. The locals were very friendly, and we marched a couple of miles along a dusty road to a camp of bamboo huts.

Being the advance party for this unknown project, our job for the next few months entailed unloading trains, clearing the jungle for future camps and for the start of the railway we were to build through to Burma. We cut bamboo in lengths of 30ft and around 4" in diameter. These were used for the main structures of the huts then we lashed thinner bamboo cane continually along the sloping roofs which we then covered in attap, the same as tiling a roof. This was made from dried leaves and strung together to a covering about 2ft x 1ft. These made quite a good waterproof roof, provided they were tied securely and with plenty of overlap.

We were now accustomed to the life and working day of a coolie on an average of three bowls of rice a day. We had been ordered by the Japanese to dig a series of monsoon drains around the huts and before long we were to find the reason why.

The day's work started at daybreak, and each morning a fatigue party was sent about a mile down the road to collect the breakfast rice in large wooden boxes with shafts on each end. One morning it was my duty to rouse the party, and take them down to collect rice. The previous evening, my mate who slept next to me on a bamboo platform about 18" off the ground, had been eating some sugared rice and a certain amount of sweetened crumbs had dropped around him. During that night the monsoon started, the river rose about 30ft flooding the entire camp. I awoke to a strange noise of water swiftly passing through the hut. I lit my lamp which consisted of a piece of string in a tin of coconut oil. I noticed a moving bundle next to me. It was my mate still snoring, but covered in a seething mass of large red ants. I turned and dangled my legs over the edge with the intentions of putting my boot on. I say boot, because the other had disintegrated a few weeks before and I had wired the sole on to an existing one. I believe half a loaf is better than none. I grappled around the dim light and eventually found it. It had floated down the hut and had finally got wedged. By this time I was a bit late so I grabbed for it. I had just tied around my piece of string when I felt a stabbing pain, like a hot knife in my foot. When I got my boot off again, I found a large scorpion had taken refuge in it. I promptly dealt with it and I urinated on the sting. We managed to get to the cook house down the road but by now we were well behind time. We broke into a trot and passed the guard into the camp. We made a bee line towards the huts. The whole camp area was by now covered in about 3ft of water. Two of the chaps in the front shafts disappeared, they had gone straight into the monsoon trenches. Naturally the chaps on the back and the boxes of rice became submerged in the water. That morning the rice was a little stodgier and a little darker than usual, but as it was not quite daybreak, the saying 'what the eyes don't see the heart don't grieve' applied.

During the next couple of months we had cleared quite a few miles northwards for the railway and the next camp site, which was eventually to become one of the largest camps, known as Chung Kia. The cemetery grew very rapidly. It is still there, beautifully maintained. This camp also became the main railway base camp for all the future thousands of P.O.W.s and native civilians to be brought up from Malaya and Singapore, many of whom were made to march the whole journey. Many were in a very bad way on arrival and consequently died before moving up north, and it became a full time job for a detailed party to work as grave diggers.

All the time the poor diet began gradually to take its toll, and the number of men fit to work began to shrink, dysentery and malaria being most prevalent and to remain throughout our captivity, beriberi was also rife through the lack of vitamin B, and the first sign of this was found in the swelling of ankles. They would puff up to two or three times their normal size, so when a finger was pushed into them, the indent would stay, showing like pressing a piece of dough.

Pellagra, septic scabies and tropical ulcers were another external problem. It was a common sight to see a couple of hundred men scrubbing their backsides with one bucket of water with the last few dredges of sulphur in it, after which they paraded up and down in the sun. We found that the sun did them good but dried them up. Sitting became very painful as they would split open again and you would stick to your seat. Flies became our biggest enemy, I would say myself worse than mosquitoes. We had all been subjected to several bouts of malaria by now, so we were past worrying about mossies, but flies became a real pest. When I say flies, 90% were bluebottles. Therefore, on every little spot of scabies, every ulcer on your body, there would be, except for night time, hundreds of these fighting to settle on you. This was most unpleasant but like everything else you got used to it in time.

I remember one day in particular, I had at the time a dozen or so ulcers on my legs. These would start with a simple scratch from bamboo or even a bite; as the body was so run down, within a couple of days the punctured skin would develop into a hole sometimes the size of a golf ball. Before mine got to that stage, I made up my mind to treat them methodically twice a day with my own remedy. The only material I had to use was an old woollen sock. This I cut into about six pieces making them into pads, then boiling them up in an old billy can with a few lumps of rock salt in the water; when they had been boiled, I would screw out the surplus water and plonk them on. After several goes at each wound, I would wrap my legs in banana leaves like gaiters. This was the only form of covering available to try and stop these bloody blue bottles from settling on them, thus saturating the wound with maggots.

Many doctors let the maggots clean out the pus, then they would pick them out with tweezers and try to keep them free from further infection. Many chaps had diphtheria ulcers apart from normal diphtheria, also many had their testicles infected. Every disease, internal or external was 99% lack of vitamins and protein etc. and it was a challenge unrivalled I should think to any other medical staff in any campaign. By this time medicines, drugs, dressings were down to usually an odd jar of Epsom salts, a bottle of acriflavine and maybe a few dozen quinine tablets, no dressing, and a few surgical tools. The same applied to personal kit. My total wealth at this period amounted to half of a towel that had worn to handkerchief thinness, one blanket that had more or less rotted away with continually getting boiled every week to kill the lice, and the most important I reckon, my 'titfer' which I never let out of my sight.

Nearly everyone by this time was down to a single article of clothing, the G string, which in this climate proved to be a very handy garment. Later on, I thought I had invented a new trend in fashion in an old shirt tail with the bottom twelve inches tied round the waist, little did I know then that thirty years later these would be the latest trend in civilization. My reason for this was that I found it kept the flies off my Khyber Pass and it didn't get stuck to the septic sores when you sat down. I don't suppose I looked very elegant while using a shovel or pick, but you can't have it all ways. Other garments which we made and wore only in the drier season and which have since become popular in civilization, are the clip clop shoes. These we carved out of solid wood with the strap made of either a bit of webbing or motor tyre; another form of footwear was about 12in. of motor tyre on each foot tied around the ankle with string. Quite honestly there wasn't much point in wearing footwear or clothes if we had them to wear, especially in the monsoon season, or standing in the river pile-driving the bridges, in the dry hot season: your own sweat would rot them in no time.

En route to Singapore I had purchased some hairclippers and scissors on our call at Durban. I don't really know why, I had never done hairdressing before, just thought maybe they would come in handy, because I liked a short back and sides every week. As it turned out, they were to stand me in good stead: at a rough estimate, I gave about 10 to 15 thousand haircuts, and I used the same clippers up to a couple of years ago to give mates a trim up at work. Shaving was more of a problem. I solved this by getting a keen edge on an army dinner knife and stropping it on an old webbing belt. This was fine for myself but it wouldn't stand up to a couple of dozen bearded chins a day. I had a Ronson lighter my mother had bought me for a birthday present before coming abroad, and I decided to flog it to a Thai in exchange for a cut throat razor. The lighter was of little use, as a smoke was a very rare pleasure, and by charging 5 cents for two shaves it meant a step towards survival, the haircut was done free. Sentiment is of little use in times like this, if a chap was dying of malnutrition with a gold wedding ring on his finger it would not help him survive, whereas he could get some extra nutrition by flogging it. I'll always remember getting a dog cut up into chunky lumps and roasting it on bamboo skewers, I offered some to one chap and he reckoned he couldn't have looked his dog in the face when he got home. I said he might not get home to do that if he didn't get some protein down – as it happened he didn't.

There was one thing it was impossible to do and that was to try and impress upon a person the view that this suffering wouldn't go on for ever. Once a chap looked at it in this light, you couldn't do much for him. To me every day I survived I reckoned on it being a day nearer home. Although I say home, I very rarely thought of it. It was a sure way of breaking a person down. One blessing was that we worked on average ten to twelve hours a day; on the tenth day we had a yasme day, or rest day. The first task on a rest day was for every prisoner to kill 100 flies after which we would often unload a few trains. After a boil up of my belongings I would get down to a session of Sweeney Todd haircutting. Night time we would have a sing song. The Japanese used to say we were mad. They would drive us into the ground working all day, and they could never make out what we had to sing about, but the important thing was, we had our minds occupied and this is of the greatest importance in helping to minimize the thinking time. Most of us still tried our best to keep as clean and tidy as circumstances allowed, although soap was a very rare commodity. We always had the river within walking distance for a wash. This really was our life saver as it was our only source of drinking water also. There was the occasional body floating past but we kept strictly to boiling all water for consumption; later when cholera broke out, nobody received any rice until they had sterilized their mess tin and eating irons in a can of boiling water outside the cookhouse.

At first, we took turns to make sure this was methodically done, but when several score began to die every week with this disease carried in water, it didn't need any more emphasizing and this ritual was carried out until the end of captivity. There was one rule this taught us, and that was, the worse the conditions the greater the need for strict hygiene. Mind you, after you have been talking to friends lying around you, almost skeletons, having simply passed everything through them and vomited to a corpse, if that doesn't make your habits careful, nothing will. The only safe disposal of these victims was by burning and from this time onwards a party was detailed to collect the bodies each morning, cut a tree trunk and secure it to the elephant, then drag it down to the bridge. Usually you were working in swamps and each time the elephant heard you shackle a tree on he would fill his trunk with a load of slime, put it through his legs and shower you with it. The chain hung under his rear legs so you can see it was rather dodgy crouching down in the mud to do this. I had shifted a dozen or so trees and bent to shackle another, when I felt what I thought a rabbit punch on the back of the neck. Instead, the elephant had decided to crap on me. Normally these animals were very placid but as they were like us, grossly under nourished, they resented their heavy task, hence the muck slinging. The different precise jobs the elephants could do in the jungle made circus elephants look dim in comparison.

Working parties on bridge building soon had a further hazard to cope with, as these became regular targets for the Yanks and our bombers. From the first task of working in the river pile-driving to the final job of laying the rail track across the finished bridge, it was a pretty hazardous job. The piles were driven in the river bed with the aid of a tripod, and about a dozen chaps on each rope to heave up the hammer. All orders on rollcalls and numbering had to be done in the Japanese language, therefore the calling of numbers to keep the rhythm of the hammer in time sounded very like the old slave gangs. 'Ichi, nee a sunyer' being one, two three. When the timing went wrong or the tripod toppled over, we were ordered in line to file past a Japanese who would belt you across the head, usually with a rifle butt or a pick handle. This was an everyday ritual on all the tasks, so it became more of a laugh. More often or not the Japanese would be shortish and would stand on a log to be able to reach the height of our heads. Often he'd get in such a frenzy he would over-balance and finish up covered in mud. The best thing was to take these petty bangs and not let them see it hurt, but more important not to lose your temper, if you did you would be on a losing wicket.

What with working in the water and lack of nutrition, our feet would often swell up and be puffed to twice their size. They were pretty painful especially when someone dropped a log or something on them, apart from the walk to and from camp, which was often three or four miles. When the bombing of bridges became quite regular, we were in a vulnerable position, either stuck in the water, or as the bridge proceeded we would be in a precarious position on it, so when they did drop a lot, it was just luck whether we got it. Many of my comrades were unfortunate, but we realised these pilots had to cut the Japanese supply line to Burma. Mind you, we had to work on through the night on many occasions to repair the damage, but at least we knew the Japanese were beginning to be harassed. Often they disappeared for quite a time during these raids, in fact they were more worried by them, than we were.

At one camp where cholera was pretty bad, the fear of cholera. If you had sudden stomach pains or sickness they would keep well away from you, and before you were allowed near their camp you would have to be well disinfected from head to foot.

At one camp where cholera was pretty bad, the Japanese commandant would not allow his troops to drink alcohol, so on their rest day they would go down the line to the mobile brothel for their little bit of geisha. On returning they would slip into our camp with a few dozen bottles of saki (rice whisky) and ask me to keep them in our camp's rice store. After dusk they would creep over to the store and sit in the dark eating raw garlic and drinking. As they emptied each bottle they would ask us to bring another, so within an hour they would be pretty well canned. Then we would produce our specials; we had, beforehand, half emptied a couple of dozen bottles and filled them up with water straight from the river which was the main source of cholera. From then to the time they finished their session, we worked these on them, saying good health. We usually made around a dozen bottles which we would flog back to the natives, and the Japanese would buy them back off them on their next rest day, providing they weren't down with sickness.

Each month that passed meant fewer men fit for work. As the diet became less more men became sick. The Japanese would only supply half ration of rice for sick persons, as this was often over 50% it brought the overall camp's ration down greatly. We always pooled everything and shared equally as a sick chap's needs were often greater than a fit man's. Although I say fit, half fit would be more appropriate as nobody went a couple of weeks without malaria or dysentery, skin ailments, ulcers and beriberi were a part of life. Every couple of weeks a Japanese medical officer would come around and turn everybody out on to the compound. He would get our camp medical officer and usually try to talk him into passing more men fit for work. These medical officers stood their ground, often being badly beaten because of it. Unfortunately, the Japanese were holding the nap hand, and providing you could stand you were out navvying; even stretcher cases were carried out at times, put by the railway, given a hammer and told to break up rock for ballast to be used between the railway sleepers. The sad thing for doctors on the railway was that there was very little they could give you as they had little if anything in the way of dressings or drugs.

Bamboo became a very useful commodity and it was in abundance – in all the camp's buildings, toilets, hospitals, and stretchers, crutches, bed pans and bottles. We even built a water supply pipe from large diameter bamboo, from a well to one hospital over a distance of about two miles. We knocked the dividing section out inside the bamboo with a smaller diameter bamboo, then joined the lengths of about 30 feet together, inserted in blocks of wood, bored out to make a union. The hospital lay in the valley, so we made bamboo trestles to even up the line. It proved a great success, as two men on the well could easily maintain constant water, saving a lot of carrying. Bamboo leaves were about the only food the elephants had, in peace time they had several pounds of Guala Malacca 'sugar' every day with their diet, for the energetic work they did.

The only snag with bamboo canes was that they were a favourite place for bugs breeding inside the huts, and also you only needed a scratch from bamboo and it was a certainty to go into an ulcer. Young bamboo shoots made good eating, but you had to give them two or three boil ups, changing the water each time. This was very important as the shoots were covered in fine silky hairs, almost invisible, but if you should get these in your throat there was a likelihood of choking to death. The other very useful local commodity, the banana leaf, was very handy for wiping your Khyber pass, especially when you went sometimes twenty or thirty times in twenty-four hours.

A common sight every day was a line of several dozen men on sick parade with a piece of banana leaf containing a stool (a specimen of crap). This was normal procedure with dysentery, one famous treatment was to crush up charcoal to a powder, and eat a pint mug full, if it didn't choke you it sometimes bound you up. Banana leaves are often about four feet long by about 16" wide so they were quite a size. The local natives dried these and rolled their cigarettes up in them. Paper of any kind was very seldom seen. Sometimes a bit of native home grown tobacco would get into camp, half of the mixture was bits of charcoal. What with the strength of the weed and the charcoal crackling and sparkling it was more like smoking a firecracker. Many Bibles finished up as cigarette paper, and the taste of printing didn't make the flavour any better. Some folk may not agree with using a Bible for such purposes, but after all it is only a manufactured article. I once asked a padre what he thought of it and he was of the same opinion.

I personally have never read the Bible, and I did not see why I should start then. One thing I did know was that it wouldn't bring back many of my personal friends who had died slowly and painfully through brutal treatment by other religious people who prayed twice a day. I often did wonder if they prayed for their sins to be forgiven or for some more prisoners to die. I suppose they must have had some loved ones somewhere.

Food was the main topic of conversation most of the time, and unless you have experienced a long period without vitamins and protein you would never realize the ultimate results which appeared within a very short time. We were lucky in so far as our main diet of unpolished rice contained a small percentage of vitamin B. We never dared to wash it before cooking for fear of losing any polishings in the process, in spite of it also containing a fair amount of weevils and rats' dirt. In some camps a few sacks of rice polishings were to be found. Luckily I used to be able to stomach this when available. It was like a mixture of sawdust and grit, and most chaps found it difficult to consume. Polished rice which we get in this country, has had the polishings removed so that it looks white and more palatable, but unfortunately it has mostly only starch left in it. The same applies to most modern snow-white bread against the old fashioned chaffie bread.

Beriberi was first diagnosed in a Java civilian prison before the war. The medical officer could not make out why chickens kept by prison officers became very weak and had difficulty in walking, whilst chickens kept by natives in the surrounding villages were healthy and walking normally. He eventually came up with the solution that although rice was their sole diet, the natives lived on unpolished rice which they also fed their chickens whilst the wardens, most probably thinking they were privileged by having lovely white rice with the vitamin B removed and which they also fed their chickens, became subject to the disease.

It seems strange to process a commodity to make it look better, extracting the most beneficial part and very likely making it dearer. The only treatment advised for beriberi was to try and find a special jungle weed, boil it and hope it would reduce some of the swelling. Lack of protein was even harder to combat, so we resorted to many species of meat that we chanced to catch, in fact anything alive – dog, cat, cobra, monkey, elephant, rodents and smaller game such as flying ants. The Japanese always had a herd of buffalo for fresh meat for their own troops, and usually we had to slaughter them as required. Often the offal would look a bit suspect and as they were inclined to be a bit fussy, they would order us to bury the carcase and offal, which we would dig up for a blow out, as soon as night fell.

Another bonus that came at times was when the Chinese and Japanese had a funeral, they would shower the grave with gifts of food to send them on their way. If we hadn't had it the vultures would. Funny ideas some people have of death. I suppose it is the most complex thing in life, but I reckon it is the one thing we are all faced with, and nobody knows where you go. Many times I thought the door was opening for me, but with a bit of extra will power, I managed to lock it. Many chaps by this time suffered with night blindness due to lack of vitamin A. Luckily I was not too severely handicapped by this, most probably due to my eating anything that was edible, never mind the taste. Before packing down at night one of us, who could see better, would line up the not so good and lead them out to the bogs. These were long slit trenches well away from the huts, about six feet deep with bamboo across to crouch on with a space here and there. Within a couple of days, these would become a seething mass of maggots which would find their way up in to camp. As the camps were in the darkness of the jungle, often some chaps would go out during the night, couldn't see where to tread and finish up in the bog up to their neck in crap.

It's a good job that nature seems to give you a greater sense of humour, to meet the greater hardships; when somebody had been retrieved from the bog you would usually say something, like calling him a stinking bleeder.

I often think that a lot of people around these days are a miserable lot, and yet you can go and see people bedridden, paralysed or blind and they always have a smile and a cheerful word. It sometimes takes a bit of hardship to bring the best out in people but I am convinced it makes one appreciate things better later on.

By now quite a few kilometres of railway banking had been completed, and although it should have been left to settle for a long period, the Japanese had one aim, to get the lines laid and trains running up from the south with supplies for their troops in Burma. Consequently, the first train up was very much like a scenic railway. It was well laden with sleepers and lines, I sat on top of an open truck with an elderly colonel. It was around midnight and the full length of the train had just got half way over a three tier wooden trestle bridge with a pretty fast flowing river under it. Suddenly we got into swaying motion and before long we came to a sudden jolting halt. There were Japanese yelling and panicking, and the timbers of the structure were creaking. Every now and then there would be a large splash of falling sleepers. After ten minutes or so things settled down a bit and we were told in pidgin English that the engine had come off the track, and myself and a couple of others had to take two jacks weighing about one hundredweight each, and crawl along the bridge and jack it back on the line. There was about a 12 inch ledge to crawl along, which made it a slow and tedious job. After about four hours of abuse and a few clouts we succeeded in getting it back on. I wasn't sorry when the train reached the other side. Unfortunately this became quite a regular hazard in future trips. With trains came another regular task of cutting down timber and splitting up the logs to half metre lengths for fuel. These would be stacked at intervals along the track. As with all other daily jobs there was a specified daily amount to do per man.

They suddenly had a brainwave to dig a well by the track side for the engines to take on water. Three of us were to dig and a couple of Chinese were to work the hand winders, pulling up the muck which we dug and loading into a large bucket. By the second day we had gone down about 15 feet and were working in water about waist high; we had filled the bucket and shouted for the coolies to take it up. After about half an hour we began to shiver, although the temperature was well in the hundreds above, we were frozen and beginning to turn blue. We didn't have the strength to climb up the rope.

By this time the water had risen to shoulder height. Suddenly we heard some chattering and laughing and the rope tightened and the bucket rose. It was then lowered for us to be taken up. Apparently our planes had bombed along that stretch of the line and the Japanese and Chinese had scarpered into the jungle. When they saw how we had puffed up, and the colour of us, they thought it a great joke. I unfortunately called them some right choice names and after a belting I had to hold a bundle of bamboo weighing a couple of stone above my head, and look up at the sun until sunset. Each time I let it drop I got a kick up the Khyber pass.

Next day I tried to get up but couldn't make it. My feet were about twice their size and I couldn't pick them up for about a week. During this time a couple of coolies were put down the well, and during their second day the walls caved in and drowned them. The Japanese couldn't wait to shore up the walls. As we went down in depth, they were always in a hurry and often dropped a clanger.

Although it was a pretty grim existence, there was some natural beauty about. Wampo, one of the camps at the beginning of the line, was a memorable occasion when from nowhere appeared thousand upon thousand of different coloured butterflies. They even settled on your head. It is impossible to visualize; it simply rained butterflies for days on end, then suddenly they all disappeared.

There were also many exotic orchids and many beautiful birds, apparently some of the rarest in the world. The one and only time I've seen a kingfisher diving was in an old swamp near the line. One elderly officer collected butterflies, and used to give you a dollar for getting orchids down from the trees. He reckoned on having one of the rarest collections in the world.

One thing I think we were fortunate in, so far as confinement was concerned, although we were closely guarded and close tabs were kept on us at all times, we were at least working to occupy the time. Funny thing is with bad times, they seem never ending whilst it is happening, but afterwards it seems like a dream. Actually, it would have been simple to escape whilst out working, but it was a mighty slim gamble on getting anywhere before you would either perish with disease, or starvation. Also there was a reward to the Thais for any prisoners captured. There were very few who attempted this. Those I knew of were all captured within days, and made to dig their own graves, they were lightly tied to a stake, so on being shot their bodies would slowly fall into the grave, and we were not allowed to bury them. This ritual was to rub it in that they didn't approve of escaping. The vultures would soon make short work of the body. Although these birds are very inelegant to look at, like everything else in this world, they seem to have a useful purpose. The same applies to ants. They too will make short work of cleaning up any dead flesh, in fact when the large red ants dropped from felled trees on to your body, it often felt as if they were trying to take you into their menu while you were still alive.

By now everybody was suffering regularly with all types of skin infection, mainly through lack of vitamins and bad conditions. Pellagra made the skin look more like leather and would become very dry and patchy. Ringworm and tinea, which would cause weeping around the crutch and testicles were a discomfort and this we had to live with.

Scabies also was a problem. This always seemed to be most pronounced on the John Thomas. It would really irritate and it needed quite a lot of effort not to start scratching. One of the medical orderlies gave me an old small dirty looking bottle with a few drops of liquid in it; he reckoned it would help the irritation. I shook the few drops of liquid onto my penis and rubbed it well in. Within a few seconds I was doing a war dance. He was certainly right about taking the itching away. I didn't feel anything of the scabies for about half an hour, but did I get some pain! I had visions of my chopper dropping off. When the pain ceased, a line of burn blisters appear right down the middle. It reminded me of the Pennine Way. Later that night, I was told that the bottle was a made up mixture of copper sulphate and creosote, and being the bottom of the bottle it was very concentrated. You can say that again!

Next morning I bumped into the camp medical officer, and he said smiling 'I hear you had a bit of hot stuff last night.' 'Yes I've got the marks to prove it.' 'Let's have a look,' he said. He laid it on his hand, paused, then took a rusty old needle pinned to the pocket of his tatty old shirt. Bomp, Bomp, Bomp, he jabbed the bulbous blisters, 'That will ease them, put a bit of banana leaf round it to keep the flies off.' And I had it wrapped in banana leaf for the next three months. Within a couple of days it had all turned septic, and eventually turned to tropical ulcers. Fortunately it did heal up. It was a case of one trouble overriding another. You don't notice the first one when something else takes over.

The further the line progressed north the more meagre the rations became, especially during the monsoon session. During these periods it was quite common for the trains not to get through with rations, because of bridges and banking being washed away. In cases like this the only means of transport was the small Thai boats up the river, or alternatively, unloading the train as far as it could get. This would sometimes mean humping hundredweights of rice for several miles. This was all right provided you didn't slip over in the slime, because once you dropped it in the mud you couldn't get it up on your shoulders again. Nobody else could help you as they were also loaded, consequently it meant the Japanese guard would give you a belting first. The trouble was most of us had a job to walk even without a load on top. Many chaps by this time were more or less walking skeletons. Consequently when you placed a load on their shoulders, their legs would just buckle under them.

When we did have rice there were always different ways and various treatments to try and make it more palatable. By the time you have completed the first year of around one thousand consecutive meals of more or less just rice, it is not very appetising.

One conception the Dutch and Japanese introduced to us was Sambal. It was made mostly of chillies boiled up to a thick pulp, a small touch of this on each spoonful of rice added a bit of flavour. I reckoned it was too blooming hot to eat, but they could eat it by the spoonful. This was the only item of food I didn't get on with. Talking of food, I must mention the selection of eating utensils used throughout our captivity. A popular plate was an old hub cap off a car, or a cut down petrol tin; eating irons were often made of bamboo. I still had my service mess tin, unfortunately it was the old fashioned type made from tin. Later types were made of aluminium. Therefore, about every five or six months I would have to pinch a bit of solder off the Japanese, and solder a new bottom in, usually a bit of an old petrol tin. The corrosion resulted from continuously dipping it in boiling water to sterilize, and as soon as the tinning wore off, it would rust over and disintegrate. It also turned a drop of jungle stew into a black sloshy colour within a couple of minutes.

Every now and then we would be moved up country, as a section of line became completed. This would often mean a march of forty or fifty kilometres carrying your few bits and pieces and cookhouse gear. If it was during the monsoon season it would be a pretty hard trek as it would be through virgin jungle with many rivers and ravines to cross by crawling across a single felled tree. The old bare plates of meat would take a caning. A real hazard was bamboo stumps and you

Part of the track, on trestles, running alongside the river.

Wampo Viaduct (sometimes called Arrow Hill Viaduct), April 1947.

*Wooden bridge built by Allied POW's at Kanchanaburi on the
Burma–Siam railway*

The steel and concrete bridge over the River Kwai at Kanchanaburi on the Burma–Siam railway, destroyed by the Fleet Air Arm.

Burma–Thailand Railway. Allied prisoners of war engaged in bridge building.

wouldn't get far before your feet would be torn.

One of these moves I remember well. I had just got over a bout of malaria, and I was still pretty groggy. Night was falling on the first day out and the couple of hundred of us were strung out over about two kilometres. I paused for a breather, and I faintly heard a splash and someone groaning behind me. I had just crossed a fast running river by clutching on all fours onto a mud covered tree trunk. I had thought I was about the last in the Indian file. Hearing another groan, I returned to the river. By this time it was pitch dark. I shouted out and a faint call came from the direction of the flowing water. Groping in the slime and mud I found the tree crossing. Eventually I came across a chap who was an officer's batman. He was the worse for wear, he had slipped off the tree in the dark and was still clutching his officer's camp bed and a six gallon tea can with one hand, and holding onto a branch with the other. I tried to pull him up, without success until I realised what he was holding onto. I grabbed the camp bed and the container and slung them down the river, then with the help of his two hands, I got him back to the north side of the river. Though I only knew him casually as Cabby, I knew he was in the Company of Signals, and a London cabby before the war.

It was belting with rain still, and we were about clapped out. Our only grub had been half a mess tin of rice at dawn that day. There was no shortage of drinking water, that was coming down in bucketfuls. We had now lost contact with the rest of the party, even the rear Japanese guards had gone and left us to it.

The mosquitoes were having a really good time with our company and the usual calling of bull frogs could be heard above the rain pounding the swampy ground. Old Cabby was still a bit worried about the loss of the camp bed and other gear I'd disposed of. I told him not to worry, it was either him or the gear and he was still alive.

I decided that the best thing was to try and get a couple of hours kip. It was impossible to see and there was always a chance of walking into further hazards. We sorted out a slight rise in the ground and lay down. Funnily enough I didn't hear another sound until I was stirred by the sound of a bugle blasting reveille. I looked across at Cabby, he was still sparked out, I tried to move, but by this time the mud and slime had half submerged our bodies. I think the mosquitoes had bitten about every part of my body. I had put on a considerable few pounds of pink flesh during the night, in fact looking down I looked a bit like a pink blancmange. After waking Cabby and giving his legs a massage to try and give him a bit of circulation, we staggered in the direction of the bugle call. Within a short while we came across a couple of dozen bamboo huts with a working party of about 200 prisoners. We had actually slept about 300 metres from the camp and they informed us our party had passed through the previous afternoon. I met two or three chaps I knew in Changi, they all were pretty much the worse for wear, but we exchanged greetings the same as you would anywhere else in the world. Over a bowl of rice they told us that they had lost half their party in the last month with cholera and they had burnt much of the camp down to try and minimize the epidemic. The walking members of the camp were working nearby on a cutting, as in this part of the country there were plenty of high peaks to be overcome. Wishing them all the best, Cabby and I set off in pursuit of our party. I thought it might be a good idea to get down nearer the river which ran in the northern direction in the hope of getting a lift in one of the native boats. I didn't think Cabby would walk very far. We had only gone a few kilometres when I heard the chugging of boats heading up stream. These boats reminded me of the small pleasure boats on the Thames with a canopy on top that hold about fifty people and do trips up to Hampton Court.

I scrambled down to the water's edge and shouted to the boatman – at first he didn't want to know, but suddenly he seemed to have second thoughts and swung over to our bank. By this time Cabby had got to the bank, and we went aboard. I tried to explain that we were on the look out for a clearing in the river vicinity, where we no doubt, would find our working party. They gave us a cup of coffee, made from burnt rice.

Many Thais earned their living on the Mekong river, some by selling small items of food and merchandise. Others would go up stream and ferry down huge amounts of bamboo which they would lash together to form a raft consisting of hundreds of canes around forty or fifty feet long. They would then build a bamboo hut on the raft to live in during the journey. What always struck me was that natives in primitive places always seemed to be happy with their meagre existence. They always seem to have plenty of celebrations and it was nothing uncommon to hear music and drums beating for days on end in the jungle. Like the Chinese, they were very artistic and very clever with their hands; even funerals were very noisy musical processions.

We must have dozed off, for suddenly we awoke to the sound of Japanese shouting and bawling. We had evidently pulled alongside a small bamboo jetty. Everything existed on bamboo, it weathered well, was easy to work with, light and extremely pliable and yet terribly strong, although it actually comes under the category of grass. We thanked the boatman for his help, unfortunately one of the Japanese gave him a doing over for giving us a lift. One of our officers came along, apparently Cabby was his batman. He started to lead off about not having his camp bed the previous night. I explained that unfortunately Cabby had fallen in the river and that his bed was very likely making steady progress towards Bangkok. After a few clouts from the guards, we were allowed to have a wash in the river and a bowl of rice.

It was good to be back amongst my mates and we set to work until dusk, digging trenches for latrines. There was a strong rumour around camp that we might be getting some Red Cross supplies, and even some mail. Over the past few weeks we had seen plenty of new khaki drill shirts and shorts but the Japanese were wearing them and smoking English cigarettes. We did eventually get an issue of Red Cross supplies which worked out to one item. A small tin of bully beef to twelve men. This was the sum total and I never did get a letter until the war finished. My parents received one pre-printed card with a couple of alternate answers you put a tick to. This they received in 1944, a year after me writing it.

Darkness fell on our new camp, and we celebrated with a sing song by the light of a log fire. All the old favourites would be rendered by the participants, songs about Ned Kelly from the Aussies, native songs from Borneo and Java, Cockney songs from myself, and the old faithful from the Jocks to finish up, 'Keep Right on to the end of the Road', very appropriate, I used to always say to myself. It's a bloody long road. All in all, it was a good night, considering the only liquor was a drop of boiled water. Funny thing was I used to sing old music hall songs most of the time, even going to work and during different jobs. Even at work now I still burst into song. Some folk may think I'm bit crazy, but it would very likely help them to get rid of present day tensions you hear about if they tried it, because I don't have any trouble in this respect. After a couple of days we settled down to our old routine, digging, picking it up, carrying it, thousands of trips up the banking and tipping it out. It's a good job it was one of my main hobbies when I was a kid, digging up the back yard with spoons. Bits of old piping my father would bring home for me I would lay under ground to drain the puddles across back into the drain hole. I certainly got a basinful of my childhood hobby back as a full time occupation.

For our labour we were paid at the rate of 10 cents a day for other ranks, 15 cents, for sergeants and commissioned officers got 25 cents. Mostly the money was printed by the Japanese themselves. We were usually paid every tenth day, so it made it an even dollar, and dollar and a half for squaddies and Sergeants. I suppose that providing you were paid a few cents, you couldn't be called slaves. Sometimes it was possible to purchase a few bananas or little fried chapattis from the natives. They more or less had set prices all the way up the line, some chaps would go for the home made cigarettes when they were available to purchase. Myself, my number one buy was ducks' eggs. When I got the chance to get them, I always ate them raw, and I reckon they were worth their weight in gold.

By this time, the number of deaths and the amount of sickness began to take a heavy toll and fewer men were capable of working. The Japanese solved this problem by forcing the Asian civilians, men, women and children to trek up from Singapore into Thailand. These families were a pitiful sight, and it became quite common to find them dying, on our way to and from work. Strangely enough, their Asian colleagues would make no attempt to assist them, but they would steal their belongings, something to do with religion I believe.

Eventually our northwards bound work on the railway met up with the Aussies who had started at Moulmein and worked southwards. Around this time several thousand of us were taken back down the line to the Chukai base camp. Rumours were very strong of us being shipped to Japan. I was still in the company of several of my close friends who had managed to survive, and we all took the view that things couldn't get much worse, and after all a change is as good as a rest. At least the climate would be a bit more like home, and we would also see even a brick building or say a proper made up road again. After a couple of days we were issued with a few bits of bedraggled old Khaki winter army clothing. This is it I thought. Later that day we were told we were going on a sea voyage, also there were to be about a dozen of us to go back up the line to work on maintenance of which I was one. That buggered that, especially as all my old mates were still on the trip. Unfortunately many who went were lost at sea.

The following day, we were taken back up country almost into Burma. The contingent consisted of about forty Aussies and a couple of hundred Dutch and Javanese. We soon amalgamated together, and before many days we were like old friends. The diggers were the right lads for this camp as most of the graft was wood cutting in the teak forests. I wouldn't mind a few of the teak and mahogany trees we had to fell, cut up into half metre lengths and split for fuel, at the price of this timber today. Before very long we had a still going, and began to prepare a brew up of rice whisky for the coming Christmas.

We would have a regular sing song every night and the Aussies like me, had their own party pieces. Another Cockney and myself would take off Flanagan and Allen, one chap had the script and all the patter from one of their shows. I wonder what we looked like. I remember the patter started, 'Cold on the Embankment Tonight, Ches'. Funny, it wasn't very warm during the monsoon season standing in a threadbare G string and the rain usually dripping through the hut, but I can assure you it was still done very enthusiastically. I would also take off Harry Champion with 'Any old Iron'. The Japanese would often say, 'You English No. 1 singer.' They couldn't have a clue what I was singing about. I think the little steps and the ''ow's your father' tickled them.

The festive season of 1944 was approaching. We had prepared a real nosh up. We had during the previous months accumulated a few lumps of salted pork and other little items whilst on fatigues in the Japanese cookhouse. This job consisted mostly of water carrying from the river, but you always had your mince pies open for any bits and pieces or a bit of sugar. Sugar by the way, was used by the Japanese not in spoonfuls, but by the pound, fish, stew anything, they ate it swamped with sugar.

Christmas Day arrived, and we were given most of the day off, and around sunset we made our way to the little bamboo shack where our long awaited meal was being prepared. I carried out the ritual of dipping my old mess tin in the boiling tin of water, and proceeded to get our Christmas dinner. It consisted of a bit of rice, fried up in a drop of coconut oil, mixed in it were our bits of salt pork and bamboo shoots and a knob of sweet potato. A couple of diggers and myself sat down a few yards away. I hadn't even got to a piece of meat, when from out of the evening sky dived one of our Mosquitoes. He strafed the camp with guns ablaze. We dived for cover and in doing so my tin went up in the air. After several runs on the camp they left us in peace to resume our feast, the only trouble was to find it, although I was sitting on a log the actual ground surface was a mass of mud and bamboo leaves. By the time everyone from the cookhouse had belted past us for cover my precious meal had got well trodden in. I never did find a piece of that salt pork, so much for that blow out, but at least a bit of lead didn't find me.

Apart from our everyday work, I still used to do a dozen or so haircuts, occasionally on Japanese. They would want an 'all-off' and I wouldn't have much option other than to oblige. One day in particular a certain boisterous Jap came demanding a haircut, after which he demanded a shave which also included eyelids, eyebrows and lug holes. I proceeded to tell him in pidgin Japanese, no razor. He started creating, when suddenly an old sweat from the Argylls called out, 'Here you are Bill, you can use mine, and cut his bloody throat at the same time.'

I thanked Jock, but I said I hadn't used a cut throat razor in my life. All during this time this short-arse Japanese was shouting at me to get started. I thought, blimey, I'm right in the crap now. There was no alternative. I had a slight advantage of being used to using tools in both hands, I had no soap so I rubbed a bit of coconut oil round his gob and in it, I got round his chin and up to his ears, and proceeded round his Adam's apple when he started to shout, 'Speedo!' I did and I thought I'd cut his wind pipe. He put his hand to his throat looked at his hand smothered in blood, I thought Christ this is it, I could see his rifle with fixed bayonet standing against a nearby tree, I had visions of him putting this straight up my jaxy. Luckily I noticed he had a largish mole on his neck, and I remembered when I've been cut at the barber's how a mole bleeds. I quickly pointed to a large mole on my neck and he suddenly stopped shouting and said, 'OK, OK, very good, soldier.' He jumped up, put his hat on picked up his rifle and he went. I saw him doing guard on a working party a week later. He still had a plaster on his throat, but he never came back shouting for a shave again. In fact when I saw him at future times he appeared to give me an old fashioned look. Funnily enough, from that day on I shaved hundreds of chaps with rubbed down hacksaw blades, and army issue dinner knives stropped up on a bit of equipment webbing, and I've never cut another person since.

Most of the time I had bother with Singapore ear. This is an infection picked up in water. You get a continuous discharge, sometimes very painful. At this particular time I had a tooth playing me up for a week or two, and what with other tropical troubles I thought it time it went.

There was an Aussie pilot I was friendly with and I knew he had found a set of dentists' tools in Singapore. He didn't have a clue about teeth but he was quite a sensible chap. I approached him and he decided to have a go. I stood against a tree and another digger held my arms as there was no anaesthetist. He chose what we thought a likely pair of forceps and we started. He had forewarned me that once he had a hold of it, he wouldn't let go. The tooth appeared to be about 6" long before it came away. Although it was painful at the time, he did a beautiful job. After this, I made up a primitive foot treadle drill and apart from extractions we also did a bit of stopping using plaster of Paris as a filler.

We were now beginning our fourth year of captivity and we still had received no news from home. We could tell by the amount of bombing raids carried out by ours and the Yanks planes, that things were steadily improving on the fighting front. In the past few weeks we had to dig a very deep trench along the camp during our rest time, around six foot deep, six foot wide and the length of the camp. This did not appear to me to look very rosy, guessing what the ultimate use of this trench would be. We took the view of a possible landing by the Allied forces from Burma, and if this arose we thought best to be out of the Japanese reach for a few days until our chaps arrived. Six of us, two British and four Aussies, were to be a close knit party. We had collected a few emergency rations and water and stored them out in the jungle. We also made some bamboo spears.

We drew up a code of practice to be maintained, that who ever they met in the jungle they would be unable to tell the tale. We had realized that we couldn't involve the whole camp in this venture particularly with the different nationalities, and obviously the greater the number the bigger the risk of secrecy.

As it turned out, we never had to carry this out. Within the next few weeks we were suddenly taken back to Chukai base camp. We had been there about a week, more or less a rest we thought. We also arranged quite a large concert party on a stage built up of earth. The show was almost over when one of our officers came on stage and said the Japanese had capitulated. It took a week for it to sink in. Everybody was up talking throughout the next few nights. From that concert party night the Japanese disappeared. They had sensibly been informed before we knew it was all over. During the next days supply planes made regular trips dropping food and medical supplies. Within a week we were transported to Bangkok airport where we were greeted by the stalwart of the Red Cross, Lady Mountbatten.

From there Dakotas flew us to Rangoon. We stayed in an emergency hospital for a few days and then down to the sea. The sight of that boat anchored out there was what we had been waiting for: back to Blighty.

In the past three and a half years, more times than not the chances of making this trip had seemed a bit remote, although personally I had no doubts. We were ferried out to our Dutch liner S.S. *Boisavain* and put aboard. The next four weeks were to me, and a few others better than any millionaire's cruise, but for the majority including the crew it was an arduous and messy trip. I should say that it was a bit of a rough voyage. You could not put a foot anywhere without slipping in somebody's misfortunes. There were about forty chaps to each mess table and at meal times, on my table there were myself and a mate. Every meal we would draw the food from the galley for forty, and sit there on our tod tucking in. This carried on until we reached Suez, and then a few more were able to join us, as their stomachs became settled. Another chap and myself worked a few hours a day in the hairdressing salon. This was run by an Australian. He also ran a gift shop on board selling eastern leather goods. He offered us both a full time job, but we had a much greater priority in view. Every afternoon we would take our blankets up on deck to get a sleeping pitch in the fresh air. We were a couple of days out of Liverpool when I went down with a bout of malaria. During the next couple of days I slept on the mess table. I well remember waking up and hearing sirens of every craft blasting, as we berthed in Liverpool. Chaps were coming down from deck and crying their eyes out. I asked them what was going on, then I could hear a military band playing on the quayside. A couple helped me up on deck to the strains from the band playing 'It's a long way to Tipperary'. I soon found out what the tears were about.

We stayed in Liverpool that night, and next day we travelled by train to London. From there we were transported by volunteers in private cars right to our home. Then I knew I'd made it. A bit the worse for wear maybe, and minus a bit of weight, but I'm sure a lot wiser.